Ayron V. Pinheiro de Assunção

Green and Social Accounting in Sustainability Policy

AF154721

Ayron V. Pinheiro de Assunção

Green and Social Accounting in Sustainability Policy

Green and social accounting indicators

Imprint

Cover image: www.ingimage.com

This book is a translation from the original published under ISBN 978-613-9-74000-0.

Publisher:
Sciencia Scripts
is a trademark of
Dodo Books Indian Ocean Ltd. and OmniScriptum S.R.L publishing group

120 High Road, East Finchley, London, N2 9ED, United Kingdom
Str. Armeneasca 28/1, office 1, Chisinau MD-2012, Republic of Moldova, Europe
Printed at: see last page
ISBN: 978-620-6-23935-2

SUMMARY

CHAPTER 1

1. General Summary

With globalisation, policies aimed at achieving development or sustainability have become a call for many in recent decades. A series of events have been taking place, bringing important measures back to the political scene. To measure the impacts on the various variables related to the growth and development of society, indicators such as the Human Development Index (HDI) and the Environmental Sustainability Index (ESI) have emerged, a theme that contemplates the research line Society, Environment and Sustainable Regional Development. The general objective of this work was to identify the level of sustainable development of 79 municipalities in the state of Mato Grosso do Sul, taking into account variables that aggregate the environmental, economic and social issues. To achieve this objective, the methodological procedure consisted of a secondary data collection in the year 2016 in several public agencies, including IBGE, SICEA, which is a reference instrument for the environmentally sustainable economic growth system. The methodology consisted in the use of estimating through the environmental social balance sheet by means of selected indicators, the impact and performance of environmental quality, applied to the economic, social and environmental information of each municipality of the MS. With this measurement we will evaluate the level of sustainability of each municipality. As a general result, it is possible to identify and hierarchise the cities with the best performance in each dimension. Similarly, the SDI in the state of MS was also analysed, with the ranking of the 10 municipalities that presented the best sustainable development index and the worst index. **Keywords**: Sustainability indicators, environmental social accounting, growth and development, Mato Grosso do Sul.

CHAPTER 2

2. General Summary

Indicators of green and social accounting in sustainability policy in the state of Mato Grosso do Sul, Brazil. With globalisation policies aimed at achieving development or sustainability has become a call for many in the last decades. A series of events has been taking place, re-measuring the important political scenario. In order to measure impacts on the various variables related to the growth and development of society, indicators such as the Human Development Index (HDI) and the Environmental Sustainability Index (ISA) have emerged, thematic area that includes of the research line Society, Environment and Sustainable Regional Development. The general objective of this work was to identify the level of sustainable development of 79 municipalities in the state of Mato Grosso do Sul, taking into account the environmental, economic and social variables. In order to achieve this objective, the methodological procedure consisted in a collection of secondary data in 2016 in several public agencies, among them IBGE, SICEA, which is a reference tool for the system of environmentally sustainable economic growth.

The methodology consisted of the use of selected environmental indicators, the impact and performance of environmental quality, and the economic, social and environmental information of each MS municipality. With this measurement we will evaluate the level of sustainability of each municipality. As a general result, one can identify and rank cities with the best performance in each dimension. In a similar way, the IDS in the MS state was also analysed, with the ranking of the 10 municipalities that presented the best index of sustainable development and the worst index.

Keywords: Growth and Development, Sustainability Indicators, Environmental social accounting, Mato Grosso do Sul.

CHAPTER 3

3. General Introduction

The advent of sustainability brings with it the multiple interactions of all sectors of the economy and the environment due to the growing severity of environmental problems and the increasing awareness of the repercussions of these problems.

While conventional national accounts take into account a fundamentally based analysis of economic growth they reflect only the level of activity of the economy disregarding issues related to the utilisation of environmental assets traded during the process of transformation of goods and services from these activities. The System of Environmental Economic Accounting (SEEA) contains internationally agreed standard concepts, definitions, classifications, accounting rules and tables to produce internationally comparable statistics on the environment and its relationship with the economy. The structure of the SAICS follows an accounting framework similar to that of the System of National Accounts (SNA) and uses concepts, definitions and classifications compatible with the SNA to facilitate the integration of environmental and economic statistics.

Environmental accounting refers to modifications to the System of National Accounts to incorporate the use or depletion of natural resources (IUCN, 1998). There are significant differences between the applications of Environmental Accounting in the public and private sectors. In the public area, the main interest is the modification of the Systems of National Accounts (SNA), internalising environmental assets and liabilities in their balance sheets and other statements, as well as the use of the data thus made available for the purpose of external control or jurisdictional control. In the private sector, its use has been progressively implemented by transnational companies, essentially interested in presenting a satisfactory image to their shareholders, consumers and pressure groups that are very active in their countries of origin.

In this new context, prospective analyses to anticipate impacts and identify strategies for Brazilian development are fundamental for sectoral and regional prospective studies that support the improvement of public policies by providing subsidies to strategic programmes that take into account environmental sustainability issues.

Within this approach, the possibility of constructing indicators to account for issues such as green national accounting and sustainability indicators are of fundamental importance to measure the impacts of economic activity on the environment and on society as a whole in the state of Mato Grossso do Sul.

Thus, the diagnostics generated offer the decision-making bodies of sectoral prospective studies subsidising the improvement of public policies and strategic programmes, expanding the advice and cooperation of the SCN with other relevant government bodies, influencing the evaluation and formulation of public policies and government programmes.

The general objective of this work will be to determine and analyse the level of sustainable development of the 79 selected municipalities of MS based on the parameters of green accounting, using the indicators of the social balance sheet, selected environmental balance sheet of the year 2016. The specific objectives are to hierarchise the selected municipalities and to apply integrated economic accounting systems to the sectoral and regional sustainable development of the state.

CHAPTER 4

4. Literature Review

4.1 Green and social accounting

In order to mitigate the impact of externalities and promote equitable actions in relation to the environment, in the 1970s, the United Nations (UN), with the aim of promoting the inclusion of the environment in studies and discussions on the core of sustainable development, created the United Nations Environment Programme (UNEP) and held the United Nations Conference on the Human Environment in 1972.

In terms of the concept of sustainable development, according to the World Commission on Environment and Development (WCED), this is defined in the Brundland report in 1987 as "sustainable development is development that meets the needs of current generations without compromising the ability of future generations to meet their needs and aspirations" (WCED, 1987).

In search of a balance to ensure the harmonious development of the human species and the environment for the current and future generation, that is, the guarantee of sustainability, it is necessary to understand the relationship between man and the environment, and how this relationship occurs over a certain period.

Thus, DEMETRIO *et al.* (2009) reports that the development model of cities around the world is physically connected to the use of energy and resources from nature. This means that it is necessary to seek production mechanisms taking into account environmental issues, since these have a connection with the other variables.The preservation of natural capital (environment) is important for the maintenance of sustainable growth, a better living condition for man, making evident the need for an economic system connected with the environment, where the economic and environmental systems participate in a larger and non-individual exchange process.

However, conventional national accounting systems cannot measure the uses and resources of traded natural assets or even the degradation of natural capital (UN, 2014).

Thus, the productive economic system, during the production process of a given good or service, does not account for the costs of externalities generated in the production process by conventional methods.

As COASE (1960) already noted, the commercialised values of goods and services do not include the costs of externalities that production and consumption processes may have for society as a whole.

For DUCHIN (2009), fuels, various minerals, land, water and other components of the environment are crucial to the maintenance of life, directly and indirectly through their respective roles in the production of goods and services.

Understanding this flow of inputs, such as energy and water, and outputs, which can be social welfare itself, is crucial if countries are to develop sustainably, allocate their resources optimally and preserve the environment.

In a complementary way, MIRANDA (1980) states that environmental problems, as a rule,

6

are originated by economic activities and, even so, it is hardly treated within a single analytical framework.

For the measurement of the externalities of the regional production system, with respect to the environment and a single basis of analysis, the theory of the input-output matrix developed by LEONTIEF (1946) will be used, which sought to study how the economic sectors of a given economy relate and connect with the environment.

From this methodology, several applications in dealing with environmental problems were developed based on the input-output matrix technique, such as the works of ISARD (1972); LEONTIEF (1970); MILLER and BLAIR (2009).

In Brazil, some of the attempts to systematise environmental accounting have come from MOTTA (1995) and YOUNG *etal.* (2000). MOTTA (1995) offers a clear and complete account of the subject of environmental accounting, presenting a detailed dimension of the theoretical and methodological aspects.

MOTTA (1995) states that environmental satellite accounts expand the analytical capacity of National Accounts by offering a physical counterpart of economic activity. Thus, accounting for environmental losses represents measuring the negative cost on the environment of economic activities. In addition, it measures the service provided by the environment is added to the product as environmental output.

YOUNG *et al.* (2000) goes further by stating that using only the conventional accounting of National Accounts is weakened when the sustainability of economic activities is based on the exploitation of natural resources is not taken into account.

For Young *et al.* (2000) sustainability, understood as the ability to exploit resources now without jeopardising future levels of activity, involves a much broader time perspective than the National Accounts are able to handle. They also state that introducing this new dimension into the calculation of outputs produces corrections in the treatment of natural resources within the National Accounts.

4.2 Experimental Ecosystem Accounting Method

This model was developed by the *System of Environmental Economic Accounting* (SEEA) and is based on the framework of ecosystem accounting adopting a different perspective of accounting.Ecosystem accounting adopts a spatial approach and assets are delineated into spatial areas containing a combination of biotic, abiotic components and other features that work together. In a sense, environmental issues had their incorporation in the 1960s in economics as a critique of the overemphasis on the goal of growth at all costs and the limit of conventional economics to solve the problems that escape the market. This critical tone is clearly emphasised by the postulates of Ecological Economics pointed out by MARTINEZ ALLIER (1999):

"Ecological economics offers a critique of conventional economics and also

7

provides instruments to explain and judge human impact on the environment; ecological economics considers intergenerational issues but also distributional conflicts within the current generation. Thus ecological economics is the study of human ecology, which necessarily involves different disciplines (MARTINEZ ALLIER, 1999)."

Ecosystem assets provide ecosystem services, which are the contributions and benefits of ecosystems to economic and other human activities. SEEA experimental ecosystem accounting has a system of accounts that presents a coherent and comprehensive view of ecosystems:

Ecosystem extent account: This account serves as a common starting point for ecosystem accounting. It organises information on the extent of different types of ecosystems within a country in terms of area.

Ecosystem condition account: This account measures the overall quality of an ecosystem asset and measures key indicators, the state or functioning of the ecosystem in relation to its naturalness and its potential to provide ecosystem services.

Monetary Asset Account: This account records the monetary value of opening and closing stocks of all ecosystem assets within an ecosystem accounting area additions and reductions to these stocks.

Thematic accounts: This set of accounts, covering land, water, carbon and biodiversity accounts, are stand-alone accounts on topics in their own right and are also of direct relevance in measuring ecosystems and assessing policy response.

In a schematic way, we can visualise the reasoning of this method in figure 1.

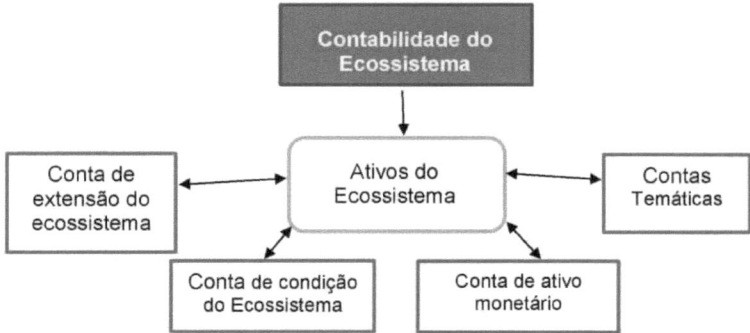

Figure 1 - Ecosystem accounting model.

The objectives of this accounting model is to synthesise measurement, concepts derived from various disciplines. It is intended to be used to encourage and support the work of ecosystem accounting in facilitating the exchange of related experiences for the testing of its variables.

This reflects the fact that ecosystem accounting is a relatively new and emerging field of measurement and is considered experimental. However, this method of accounting builds on findings in well-established disciplines such as official statistics, indicators and the field of environmental accounting.

4.3 Sustainability and environmental management

Currently, there is a growing awareness of environmental aspects and the notion of sustainable development, since this concept, in addition to being used in political speeches, has gradually been incorporated into public policies in both the economic and social spheres. "Thus, the theme of sustainability is institutionalised through environmental planning and management, aiming to reconcile and harmonise the relationship between the supply and demand of environmental and/or natural goods" (LAURA, 2004).

For DONAIRE (1995), organisations tend to obtain economic and strategic benefits through their engagement in the environmental cause, as shown in Table 1.

Table 1. Economic and strategic benefits of adopting environmental management

Economic benefits	Strategic benefits
Cost savings - Savings due to reduced consumption of water, energy and other inputs - Savings due to recycling, sale and utilisation of waste and reduction of effluents - Reducing fines and penalties for pollution *Increased revenue* - Increased marginal contribution of "green products" that can be sold at higher prices - Increased market share due to product innovation and less competition - New product lines for new markets - Increased demand for products that help reduce pollution	- Improving institutional image - Renewal of the product portfolio - Increased productivity - High staff commitment - Improving labour relations - Improvement and creativity for new challenges - Improved relations with government agencies, community and environmental groups - Ensured access to the external market - Better compliance with environmental standards

Source: DONAIRE (1995).

VALLE (1995) points out that in addition to the moral persuasion that society imposes on

9

organisations to stimulate environmental control, some fiscal and economic mechanisms have also been created, capable of inducing organisations and individuals to change their behaviour and their attitude towards the environment. These include taxing or imposing fines on a "polluter pays" basis and granting benefits and tax exemptions to favour products and activities considered "natural" and "clean", among others.

In this sense, Hans (1994) argues that considering environmental demands means understanding how much ecological issues involve business and can collaborate with profits. It means that "being greener" involves numerous steps, from the manufacture of products to suppliers, customers, employees, media and the community where it is inserted, in order to obtain a synergy in the results. To this end, the author proposes an Ecological Management System, based on the seven "E's":

•   Efficiency: new technologies to be implemented in production or marketing that reduce the expenditure of time and raw materials and minimise the use of non-renewable resources.

•   Framework: the necessary adaptation of your business to current and likely new legal, policy and institutional frameworks, whether arising from government legislation or from requirements by banks, credit institutions and insurers.

•   Economy: the new level in business-to-consumer, business-to-business and business-to-international trade relations, where the ecological paradigm is being imposed with increasing force. Increasing success in the economic result.

•   Education: the requirement for constant clarification to company employees of the environmental policy adopted, in order to keep the company-supplier-public relationship up to date.

•   Engagement: education has the natural consequence of incorporating environmental issues into the corporate culture. It is important to demonstrate the strategic value of the environment to the leadership within the company. The natural consequence will be a broader and more open relationship with the public.

•   Excellence: the concern for "global quality" i.e. that ecological management covers the complete life cycle of a product - production, distribution, marketing and recycling.

•   Ethics: environmental concern must be transparent in relations with the community and be an extra factor in the company's valorisation before shareholders, government, employees, etc.

SANTOS (2010) emphasises that one of the challenges of building Sustainable Development is to create measurement tools, such as development indicators, which in this case are tools consisting of one or more variables that, associated through various forms, reveal broader meanings about the phenomena to which they refer.

In Brazil, the Brazilian Institute of Geography and Statistics (IBGE) is the body responsible for managing data on indicators. Indicators fulfil functions and report on short-, medium- and long-term phenomena, and serve to identify variations, behaviours, processes and trends, indicating needs and priorities for the formulation, monitoring and evaluation of policies and decision-making.

The World Commission on Environment and Development organises them into four dimensions: environmental, social, economic and institutional.

•   *Environmental* dimension: the environmental dimension of the Sustainable Development indicators concerns the use of natural resources and environmental degradation and is related to the objectives of preserving and conserving the environment.

•   *Social dimension:* corresponds in particular to the objectives linked to the fulfilment of human needs, improvement of the quality of life and social justice.

•   *Economic dimension: this* dimension is concerned with the efficiency objectives of production processes and changes in consumption structures geared towards long-term economic and sustainable reproduction.

•   *Institutional dimension:* this dimension includes indicators that summarise investment in science and new technologies for processes and products, as well as the role of public authorities in protecting the environment.

The task of developing indicators is a highly complex one in which the central issue lies in understanding the system (environmental problematic), what sustainability of that system is and how to measure it. It is necessary to construct this complex problematic so that the set of indicators captures and represents the scope of the study (LAURA, 2004).

ENSSLIN *et al.* (2001) proposes the use of the constructivist paradigm based on the idea of learning through participation (between actors and experts) and considering objective and subjective aspects, linking the study to the systemic and interdisciplinary approach.

4.4 Parameters in the study of sustainability: complexity and challenges

For sustainability studies, several parameters, scopes, perspectives, dimensions and indicators have been evaluated, studied, researched and analysed.

To further elucidate, parameters correspond to a quantity that can be accurately measured or assessed qualitatively/quantitatively and that is considered relevant for the assessment of environmental, economic, social and institutional systems. Indicators are parameters selected and considered alone or in combination with each other, they are usually used with pre-treatment, i.e. treatments are carried out on the original data, such as arithmetic averages, median, etc. Indices correspond to a higher level of aggregation methods, which can be arithmetic (linear, geometric, minimum, maximum, additive) or heuristic, representing decision rules (SANTOS, 2010).

For the Organisation for Economic Co-operation and Development (OECD), environmental indicators can be systematised by the Pressure-State-Response model:

•   *Pressure:* emission of pollutants, technological efficiency, environmental impact;

•   *State:* reflect the quality of the environment over a given space/time horizon;

•   *Answer:* indicators of social membership and social group activities.

LOUETTE (2007) researched the most widely used sustainability indicators in the world, arriving at the following list:

•   Human Development Index, HDI

•   Human Poverty Index, HPI

- Gender Adjusted Development Index, GDI
- Participation Measure by Gender, MPG
- Balance of Nations, NCB
- Barometer of Sustainability, BS (Sustainability Barometer)
- Dashboard of Sustainability, DS (Sustainability Dashboard)
- Ecological Footprint (EF)

- Environmental Performance Index (EPI)
- Environmental Sustainability Index (ESI)

Environmental)

- Environmental Vulnerability Index, EVI (EVI).

Environmental)

- Genuine Progress Index, GPI
- IBGE Sustainable Development Indicators, IDS
- Happy Planet Index (HPI)
- Index of Sustainable Economic Welfare (ISEW)
- Living Planet Index (LPI)

Based on Louette's work, Santos (2010) notes that the main problems related to indicators can be classified into: 1. low periodicity, small publication and few countries analysed;

2. limitations of the methodology;

3. problems in acceptance and dissemination, uncertainties and difficulty in interpretation;

4. lack of funding from government or private institutions

5. Audience restriction: some are to raise awareness among the general public others serve political or scientific purposes and cannot be understood by the general public.

A summary of the research can be seen in **Table 2**.

Table 2. Comparison of key indicators

Indicators	Data issues	Methodological problems	Acceptance issues (controversial)	
	Lack of available data, unreliable sources, data	Difficulty in replicating the methodology for obtaining the index	Difficulties of acceptance due to problems arbitrariness, commensurability	Difficulty in interpreting the results,
	not very accessible		ade ou incommensurabili	low degree of comparison

12

			ty	
HDI	X		X	
IPH	X		X	
IDG	X		X	
MPG		X		X
NCB	X		X	
BS	X	X		
DNA	X		X	
DS		X		X
EF		X		X
PPE	X	X		
ESI	X	X		
EVI	X	X		
GPI			X	
HPI			X	X
IDS	X	X		X
ISEW	X		X	X
LPI	X	X	X	X

Source: SANTOS (2010).

In this sense, BENNETTI (2006) and MEADOWS (2007), propose that an indicator should:

- Be politically relevant;
- Be meaningful in relation to the sustainability of the system;
- Allow repeat measurements over time;
- Have measurability (cost time required and feasibility of carrying out the measure)
- Be replicable and verifiable;
- Be easy to interpret;
- Have a well-determined and transparent measurement methodology;
- They must be physical, such as water, pollutants, forests, food;
- They should be provocative, leading to discussion, learning and change.

Finally, through these data, one can observe the great complexity of identifying the study parameters to evaluate projects and practices related to environmental management, including actions so recent in the national context in terms of management and research, such as the ABC Programme of the Ministry of Agriculture.

4.5 Balance of Nations method

In 2004, the Federal Accounting Council (CFC) approved NBC T 15 - Social and Environmental Information, which establishes procedures for disclosure of social and environmental information with a view to accounting to society for the use of natural and human resources, demonstrating the degree of social responsibility of the entity.

Within organisations, the fundamental role of accounting is the measurement, preparation and disclosure of economic and financial information, influencing the decision-making process. With the emergence and incorporation of sustainable development, a new challenge has arisen for those involved in environmental and social accounting.

According to KASSAI *et al.* (2008) describes a proposal called Balance Sheet of Nations (BCN), with the objective of elaborating balance sheets for countries and regions. The methodology is based on using multidisciplinary information of a qualitative nature, converting into monetary or accounting information, classifying into assets, liabilities and net worth according to the natural resources of each country.

Therefore, by analysing the NCB, it can be considered an important instrument for measuring environmental costs, with a reduction in externalities caused by human activities. (KASSAI *et al.*, *2012) The* NCB expands the boundaries of accounting, is accountable to humanity, is not limited to normative aspects, but expands to social, environmental and humanitarian concerns.

According to KASSAI *et al.* (2010), there are three possible situations to be verified by the NCB, they are:

1. Environmental Net Worth greater than zero - suggests that the country's environmental situation is in surplus, i.e. each citizen generates more than enough income to honour their commitments to the environment and there are still surplus carbon credits left over. This case corresponds to the existence of a positive externality;

2. Environmental net worth equal to zero - suggests a zero environmental situation, i.e. each citizen generates sufficient income to honour their commitments to the environment. In this case there are no externalities;

3. Environmental Net Worth less than zero - suggests that the country's economic situation is in deficit, i.e. citizens are not able to generate sufficient income to honour their commitments to the environment. In this way, it is as if the individuals of that country are taking advantage of other countries' resources, and must, for example, trade carbon credits from other nations and/or reduce their emissions. This case corresponds to a negative externality.

Graphical representation of the NCB, as shown in Figure 2.

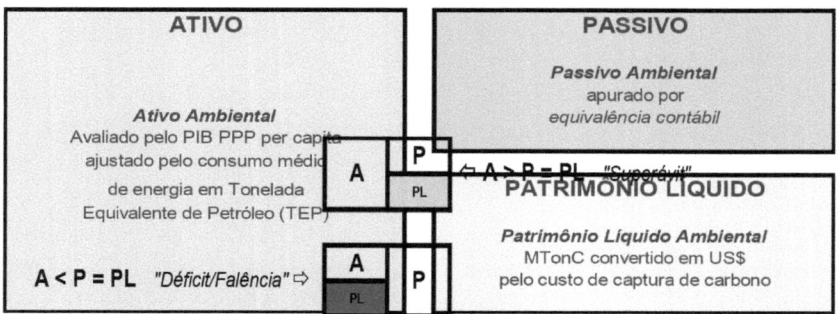

Figure 2 - Graphical representation of NCB **Source:** KASSAI *et al. (2012,* p. 79).

4.5.1 Environmental Assets

They are all assets and rights intended for or arising from environmental management activity. According to ISO 14.000 (International Organisation for Standardization) the main focus is to minimise damage to the environment through the Environmental Management System (EMS) in accordance with all environmental policies and laws.

Environmental assets can also be understood as applications and investments aimed at environmental preservation, which are intended to generate present and future economic benefits. Environmental assets are measured by GDP, which represents, in monetary values, all goods and services produced in a given country.

NCB's methodology for assessing the wealth of nations, GDP was assessed by the Purchasing Power Parity (PPP) method, which measures how much a given currency can buy in international terms, i.e. US dollars. The same was measured by PPP is publicised by the International Monetary Fund (IMF).

The GDP/PPS per capita is then calculated by dividing it by the number of inhabitants of the reference nation. Subsequently, GDP/PPS per capita is adjusted by the country's average energy consumption, measured in Tons of Oil Equivalent (TOE). One TEP is equal to 10,000,000 kilocalories (Kcal) (KASSAI et al., 2008).

The formula is realised as follows:

$$\frac{PIB/PPC \; per \; capita \; do \; período}{Consumo \; médio \; de \; Energia \; em \; TEP \; do \; período} \qquad (1)$$

4.5.2 Environmental Liabilities

In environmental accounting, a liability is a present obligation of the entity, arising from events that have occurred, the settlement of which is expected to result in an outflow of resources capable of generating economic benefits. It is related to aggression to the environment, as well as cats to compensate for damage caused.

The environmental liability is obtained by difference based on the fundamental accounting equation:

$$Assets - Liabilities = Net \; Worth \qquad (2)$$

Using the balance of Assets and Net Worth, we have the Liabilities per capita with the objective of determining how much each inhabitant of the country has of surplus or deficit in relation to environmental externalities. Representing the balance of obligations that each citizen of a country has in relation to their livelihood and preservation of the environment.

15

According to KASSAI *et al.*, (2008) environmental liabilities represent the broad set of externalities towards the environment and the Balance Sheet of Nations exposes the assets sufficient to meet their commitments, both individual and environmental.

Adjusted, we can observe the formula:

Environmental Liabilities = Environmental Assets - Environmental Net Worth (3)

4.5.3 Environmental Net Worth

The environmental heritage is composed of the set of environmental assets and liabilities. The environmental denomination is unreasonably broad, Sá (1999) emphasises that the market is environmental, nature is environmental, technology is environmental, the law is environmental, politics is environmental, that is, everything outside the heritage is environmental.

According to LIMA and VEIGAS, (2002), when one speaks of measuring environmental information, it refers to measuring, economically, the result of the impacts caused by business activities, whether positive or negative. In this sense, LIMA and VEIGAS (2002, p. 51) explain that "[...] a distinction must be made between object and attribute, that is, the object is not the measurement of pollution, but the economic impact that its externalities can cause [...]". They also comment that from the company's point of view, environmental accounting seeks to measure what its environmental assets are and how efficiently they are used, providing economic and financial information on environmental protection, preservation and recovery.

KASSAI *et al.* (2012), forests are depositories of carbon avoided in the atmosphere. For the calculation, a specific index is adopted referring to the storage potential of each of the different biomes. Carbon emissions refer to the carbon released into the atmosphere within a period of time, which comes from industrial activities, vehicles, thermal energy generation and forest fires. The variables are measured in MtC and when monetised, are converted to the carbon capture cost suggested by the United Nations (UN).

Therefore, they also define that from any angle it is analysed, Net Worth is the end result of all the effort made by the entity to allocate its assets and liabilities as efficiently and profitably as possible.

CHAPTER 5

5. Bibliographical References

CMMD. **World Commission on Environment and Development**: Our common future. Oxford: Oxford University Press, 1987. p. 28 - 59

COASE, R. H. The Problem of Social Cost. **Journal of Law and Economics,** Chicago, v. 3, p. 1-44, 1960.

DEMETRIO, F. J. C.; GIANNETTI, B. F.; ALMEIDA, C. M. V. B. Comparative Study between Sustainability and the Human Development Index. In: international workshop advances in cleaner production, 05, 2009, São Paulo. Proceedings...São Paulo: UNIP, 2009. p. 1-10.

DUCHIN, F. Input-Output Economics and material flows. In: **SUH, S. Handbook of input-Output Economics in Industrial Ecology**. Minessota: Springer, 2009. p. 61 - 218.

ISARD, W. **Ecological-Economic Analysis for Regional Development**. New York: Free Press, 1972. p. 272

KASSAI, J. R. BARBIERI, R. F. SANTOS, F. C. B. CARVALHO, L. N. G. CINTRA, Y. Balance of Nations: a reflection under the scenario of climate change. In: Brazilian Congress of Costs, 15, 2008, Curitiba. Proceedings...Curitiba: Brazilian Congress of Costs, 2008. 1 CD-ROM.

KASSAI, J. R. BARBIERI, R. F. CARVALHO, L. N. G. CINTRA, Y. The Monster Countries in the Global Climate Change Scenario according to their Balance Sheets. **Revista de Gestão Social e Ambiental**, São Paulo. v. 4, n. 2, p. 3-20, 2010.

KASSAI, J. R. BARBIERI, R.F. CARVALHO, L. N. FOSCHINE, A. CINTRA, Y. AFONSO, L. E. Accounting balance of nations: reflections on global climate change scenarios. **Brazilian Business Review**, Vitória-ES, v. 9, n. 1, p. 65-109, 2012.

LEONTIEF, W. Exports, imports, domestic output, and employment. **The Quarterly Journal of Economics**, Cambridge, v. 60, n. 2, p. 171-93, 1946.

LEONTIEF, W. Environmental Repercussions and the Economic Structure: An Input-Output Approach, **The Review of Economics and Statistics,** Cambridge, v. 52, n. 3, p. 262-271, 1970.

LIMA, D. V. de: VIEGAS, W. Accounting treatment and disclosure of ecological externalities. **Revista Contabilidade e Finanças,** São Paulo, n. 30, p. 46-53. 2002.

MILLER, R. E.; BLAIR, P. D. **Input-Output Analysis: Foundations and Extensions**. New York: Cambridge University Press, 2009. p. 10 - 65.

MIRANDA, C. R. Economy and environment: an input-output approach. **Pesquisa e Planejamento Económico**, Brasília, v. 10, n. 2, p. 601-636, 1980.

MOTTA, R. S. **Environmental Accounting: theory, methodology and case studies in Brazil**. Rio de Janeiro: IPEA, 1995. p. 28 - 72.

NU. System of Environmental-Economic Accounting 2012: Experimental Ecosystem Accounting. New York: NU, 2014. **SEAA Portal**, available at: < https://unstats.un.org/unsd/envaccounting/seearev/seea_cf_final_en.pdf > Accessed 19 July 2018.

Semagro Portal, available at: < http://www.semagro.ms.gov.br/zoneamento- ecologico-economico-de-ms-zee-ms/ >. Accessed on 19 July 2018.

PortalIPEA, available at : <http://www.ipea.gov.br/portal/index.php?option=com_content&view=article&id= 1226&Itemid=68>. Accessed 19 July 2018.

Technical Standards Portal, available at: < https://www.normastecnicas.com/iso/serie-iso-14000/>. Accessed 19 August 2018.

SÁ, A. L. Introduction to accounting applied to the natural environment. **IOB - Objective Information. Temática Contábil e Balanços**, São Paulo, n. 37, p. 69, 1999.

YOUNG, C. E. F.; PEREIRA, A. A.; HARTJE, B. C. R. **Environmental Accounts for Brazil.** Rio de Janeiro: IE-UFRJ, 2000. p. 7-34.

CHAPTER 6

6. Articles

Article I

Environmental Economic Performance of the Municipalities of Mato Grosso do Sul.

Summary

This article aims to show the economic performance caused by the main economic activities of the state of Mato Grosso do Sul, Brazil. In this context, prospective studies will demonstrate, identify the sustainability indicators of Mato Grosso do Sul for sectoral and regional studies that subsidise the improvement of public policies, assisting in the elaboration of strategic government programmes that take into account the issues of environmental sustainable development and impact parameters. Within this approach, the possibility of building indicators to measure which economic activities have the greatest performance on the environment and on society as a whole. Becoming relevant in the discussion of public policies. In addition, the diagnostics generated by the construction of synthetic indicators allow decision makers prospective scenarios regarding sustainability, supporting the improvement, evaluation and monitoring of public policies and government programmes. To this end, an aggregative indicator approach was developed to measure sustainability that evaluated the results for the 79 municipalities of Mato Grosso do Sul, revealing the main similarities and points of attention in relation to sustainability.

Keywords: Economic Performance, Indicators, Environmental Sustainability.

Introduction

Economic development and sustainability is a major concern in today's societies. Contradictions of understanding by leaders in world meetings, which aimed at generating new technologies and knowledge to assist in the living of the human race. The concept of performance in environmental economics has its pecualities; devoting considerable attention to input-output analysis in the environment covering fields with criteria to aid in decision-making. Development thinking is about reconciling economic growth with other goals, i.e. a focus on long-term thinking. This has led to a more environmentally aware and concerned society about air pollution and other sustainability issues due to the increasing severity of environmental problems and the growing realisation of the repercussions of these problems.

In the State of Mato Grosso do Sul, the regulation that instituted the Ecological-Economic Zoning should be understood as a set of actions aimed at changes in the environment, which aim at the rational exploitation of resources, the improvement of the quality of life of the population and the environmental preservation of the territory, carried out by society in conjunction with the Government of the State of Mato Grosso do Sul.

In this way, the Social Balance Sheet developed by the Brazilian Institute of Social and Economic Analyses (IBASE) expresses the social responsibility actions developed by companies, transparently showing the performance of accounting, environmental, economic and social information of the entities to their different users.

Due to the inherent characteristics of the organisation structuring process, a clearer view of the processes in which environmental costs are involved is essential, and it is necessary to elect environmental performance indicators, mitigating aggressions to the environment and consequently helping economic performance.

In this new context, prospective studies to anticipate compliance and identify strategies for the development of Mato Grosso do Sul are fundamental for sectoral and regional prospective studies that support the improvement of public policies by providing subsidies to strategic programmes that take into account environmental sustainability issues.

Within this approach, the possibility of constructing indicators to measure the responsibilities of environmental economic performance provides society as a whole with information on the situation of its regions on the one hand and on the other provides a decision-making tool in actions to correct regional inequalities.

To this end, the general objective is to measure the construction and estimation of a Sustainable Development Index within the municipalities in the state of Mato Grosso do Sul.

Material and Methods

With the publication of "Indicators of Sustainable Development (IDS): Brazil 2002", IBGE begins researching the topic sequentially, every two years. The set of information provided on the Brazilian reality in its environmental, social, economic and institutional dimensions creates a seminal contribution for decision-makers on the comprehensive panorama of the main issues related to sustainable development in Brazil (IBGE, 2016).

In its latest edition in 2016, 60 indicators were presented, most of which are divided into the four dimensions, allowing the monitoring of phenomena over time and the examination of their occurrence in the national territory (IBGE, 2016).

However, to define a state or municipal cut-off, the number of indicators would be more restricted. Unlike the magnitude of indicators available at the national level, at the regional level most of these are carried out sporadically, during census periods. From the sample surveys or those conducted systematically in the states and municipalities, the available data restrict the scope of indicators that can be used.

According to ROLDAN and VALDÉS (2002) the methodology proposed for the selection of the set of indicators to account for different regions, making it possible to compare and generate a ranking of these regions should represent the issue of sustainable development must comply with the following criteria:

• The availability and reliability of data sources;

• The most up-to-date data statistics possible;

• The representation in the analysis of three systems: natural, social and economic, with their regional importance;

A holistic approach that includes quantitative and qualitative terms.

The methodology proposed in this article should consider all municipalities in Mato Grosso do Sul, including all dimensions proposed by the United Nations Commission on Sustainable Development (CSD) and used in the IBGE's national SDI methodology. This makes the analysis more complete and the proposed regional indicators can be compared to national indicators.

The Environmental Balance Sheet (BPA), uses as a model base the Social Balance Sheet (BS), made available by the Brazilian Institute of Social and Economic Analyses (IBASE). According to CLAUDE (1997) Natural heritage accounting is a global system of records that integrates physical and monetary information into a system of relationships between economic and environmental accounts, through matrices of interrelationships that allow the information to be crossed.Following are the main social indicators to which they are divided into 7 blocks, according to PFITSCHER (2009):

a) **Basis of calculation**: These are the three pieces of financial information: net revenue, operating income and gross payroll. These figures are used to inform the impact of investments on the company's accounts, as well as to allow comparison between companies and sectors over the years;

b) **Internal social indicators:** These are the internal, compulsory and voluntary investments that the company makes to benefit and/or serve its employees (food, compulsory social charges, private pension, health, safety and medicine at work, education, culture, training and professional development, crèches and daycare, profit sharing and results, among others);

c) **External social indicators:** This part of the balance sheet presents voluntary investments, whose audience is society in general, such as projects and initiatives in the areas of education, culture, health and sanitation, sports, combating hunger and food security, tax payments and others;

d) **Environmental indicators: The** company's investments to mitigate or compensate for its environmental impacts are presented, as well as those aimed at improving the environmental quality of the company's production/operation, either through technological innovation or internal environmental education programmes. Investments are also requested in projects and actions that are not related to the business operation;

e) **Staff indicators:** This part contains information that identifies how the company relates to its internal public in terms of job creation, use of outsourced labour, number of trainees, valuing diversity - blacks, women, age group and people with disabilities - and the participation of historically discriminated groups in the country (women and blacks) in leadership and management positions;

f) **Relevant information regarding the exercise of corporate citizenship:** This refers to a series of actions related to the publics that interact with the company, with great emphasis on the internal public. The majority of these are qualitative indicators that show how internal participation and the distribution of benefits are going. This part of the balance sheet also includes some of the guidelines and processes developed in the company that are related to corporate social responsibility management policies and practices;

g) **Other information:** This space is reserved and widely used by companies to disclose other information that is relevant to understanding their social and environmental practices.

Table 1. Balance Sheet Adapted to the Environment

CURRENT ASSETS	CURRENT LIABILITIES
Available	**Loans and Financing**
Boxes	Environmental finance
Banks on a current account	**Suppliers**
Credits	Environmental Suppliers
Customers	**Obligations**
Environmental customers	Fines for environmental damage
(-) Discounted invoices	Compensation for environmental
Credits for environmental advice	damage Green taxes
Other Credits	**Provisions**
Stocks	Fines for environmental damage
Raw materials	Compensation for environmental
Products in process	damage
Finished products	Green taxes
Recycled products and by-products	**NON-CIRCULATING**
Environmental inputs	**LONG-TERM LIABILITIES**
Environmental packaging	**Loans and Financing**
NON-CIRCULATING	Environmental finance
	Suppliers
LONG-TERM REALISABLE	Environmental Suppliers
Investments Participation in other	**Obligations**
environmental companies	Fines for environmental damage
Participations in investment funds.	Compensation for environmental
Environmental	damage Provisions
Fixed Assets	Fines for environmental damage
Land	Compensation for environmental
Environmental equipment	damage Acquisitions Goods and Serv.
Depreciation, Amortisation and	Environmental Restorations
Exhaustion	**RESULTS OF FUTURE FINANCIAL**
(-) **Intangible assets**	**YEARS NET ASSETS Share Capital**
Brands	Subscribed Share Capital
Patents	**Capital Reserves**
	Profit reserve

Accumulated environmental amortisation	Legal reserve
(-)	Contingent reserve for environmental damages **Profit for the year or**
TOTAL ASSETS	**Accumulated Losses**
	TOTAL LIABILITIES

Source: Adapted from TINOCO and KRAEMER (2006).

Results and Discussion

Sustainability: conceptual and historical aspects

The concept of sustainability refers to principles such as democracy and justice; it is an easy concept to pronounce but difficult to define. In the environmental economics literature, the debate concerning the conditions of sustainability tends to be based on two concepts: "weak" and "strong" sustainability. The weak sustainability test is an intuitive rule based on the assumption of unconstrained substitution between produced and non-produced assets. An economy is considered "not sustainable" if total savings fall below the combined depreciation of produced and non-produced assets, the latter usually restricted to natural resources (PEARCE and ATKINSON, 1993, 1995).

Although environmental problems have existed for a long time, it is only recently that economic analysis has become sufficiently aware of them and their implications. This is not to say that environmental problems have been completely ignored by the various schools of economic thought. It is enough to recall their history: physiocracy placed natural resources (land) first among the factors of economic growth and the classical school considered all three factors together - land, capital and labour. However, only since the 70s of the last century, a large amount of studies and advances have emerged, mainly in the neoclassical economic line. These studies built two sciences - Environmental Economics and Natural Resource Economics.

The United Nations Organisation, through the report Our Common Future, defined Sustainable Development as: [...] Sustainable development is development that meets present needs without compromising the ability of future generations to meet their own needs (CMMAD).

So this concern has taken shape by being interpreted with a broad sense "sustainability", discerning the means of production to seek a balance.

According to RAMOS (2010), the current view of nature, enhanced by technology, inherited the domination project based on the dualism man-nature, in which the latter is instrumentalised for the benefit of the former. In other words, the stance - which has become dogma - of transforming knowledge of nature into an instrument of domination has been universalised.

The harmonious coexistence with the environment and the other species that inhabit the planet must be respected so that the value of environmental education can be preserved.

Cordani, MARCOVITCH and SALATI (1997) consider that such problems have become less important, but that new security problems such as terrorism and unemployment have attracted significant attention from leaders and society as a whole. These are short-term problems that invade agendas. In Brazil, the lack of definition of the state reform process has also reduced the priority for sustainable development actions. An example of this is the inoperability of many of the institutions dedicated to environmental issues and their coordinating bodies.

Therefore, verifying and respecting the opinion of each author, we can note that some have subjected themselves to express and establish knowledge in a clear and objective way, due to the difficulty that the subject asks, thus ensuring sustainable development is necessary to properly assess natural capital. In order not to harm future generations, it is necessary to know how much of the natural capital stock has been lost as a result of environmental degradation, how much is available today and how much is threatened by irreversible destruction in the future.

Sustainable development is a tool that will show information to aggregate controls, highlighting the impacts caused on the environment, leading to the elaboration of preventive programmes.

Sustainability indicators and indices

There is no general consensus that sustainable development is an evolutionary process that translates into the combination of three strands of a country's development for the benefit of present and future generations: growth of the economy, improvement of the quality of the environment and improvement of society.

When it comes to sustainability indices or indicators, the debate is just beginning, as there is, to date, no recipe or formula for assessing what is sustainable or unsustainable.

A sustainability index should initially refer to the relative elements of sustainability of a system (CAMINO and MULLER, 1993) and the explicitness of its objectives, its conceptual basis and its user public (ROMERO, 2004).

The construction of sustainable development indicators in Brazil is part of the international efforts to concretise the ideas and principles formulated at the United Nations Conference on Environment and Development, held in Rio de Janeiro in 1992, with regard to the relationship between the environment, society, development and information for decision-making.

However, sustainability indices imply the explanation of the mechanisms and logics acting in the area under analysis; quantification of the most important phenomena occurring in the system as shown in Figure 1.

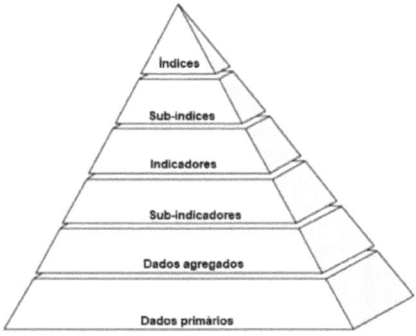

Figura 1. Level of data aggregation of a given sustainability assessment tool. **Source:** Adapted from SHIELDS *et al.* (2002).

Construction of indicators

According to JANUZZI (2005), the construction of a system of indicators for use in public policies takes place in four stages. It begins with the definition of the programme objective (1), followed by the definition of the dimensions or actions linked to the programme objective (2). From there, administrative data and public statistics are sought (3), which after being organised (4) become social indicators, as shown in Figure 2.

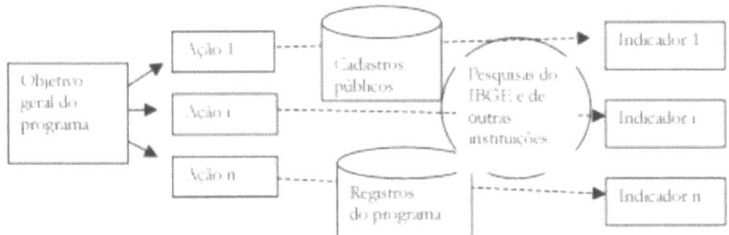

Figura 2. Construction of a system of indicators for the public policy cycle. **Source:** JANUZZI (2005).

According to JANUZZI (2005), the indicator must be intertwined with strategic planning so that it measures exactly what is proposed. For Cardoso (2005), this link between the indicator and strategic planning takes the form of a cycle, where strategic planning feeds the measurement of indicator results, which in turn uses performance information to feed strategic planning, as shown in Figure 3.

1ª Etapa:
Definição do
Planejamento
Estratégico

2ª Etapa:
Aplicação do
indicador /
Mensuração do
desempenho

3ª Etapa:
Utilização da
informação para
alimentar o
planejamento
estratégico

Figura 3. Link between indicator and strategic planning.
Source: Adapted from CARDOSO (2005).

The first stage, the definition of a programme objective, is very important to achieve the effectiveness of the indicator, because from the definition of the pragmatic objective the indicator has a well-defined conceptual basis, increasing its effectiveness (JANUZZI, 2005).

Once the programme content has been defined, the second step is to define the dimensions that will make up the indicator. These dimensions are also called "major themes", as was the case with the three indicators worked on in the Sustainable Development Index of the Ecological-Economic Zoning of Mato Grosso do Sul. At this stage, it is vital to check all the dimensions that will make up the indicator. Once verified, those dimensions that are essential to the indicator will then be detailed and those that are unnecessary will be discarded. This judgement will be the responsibility of the researcher, who should seek knowledge on the subject for such realisation (JANUZZI, 2005).

The third stage, which JANUZZI (2005) defines as the search for administrative data and public statistics, i.e. the collection of data to measure a phenomenon. Data collection can be carried out through primary or secondary data. Primary data are those unpublished data, that is, that need to be collected. Secondary data, in turn, are those data that already exist, which have been collected and made available by another researcher or institution in its own database. The main negative factor of primary data in relation to secondary data is the cost of obtaining it (financial and time) and the difficulty of obtaining the data, since most research needs to reach a large population. Secondary data are easier to access, saving time and money. On the other hand, secondary data should only be used when the researcher is sure of the reliability of these data, giving preference to data from research institutions such as IBGE or other reliable institutions.

The fourth and final step is organising the data, standardising it where necessary, using the data to measure what is desired.

The methodology for constructing an indicator is presented in Figure 4.

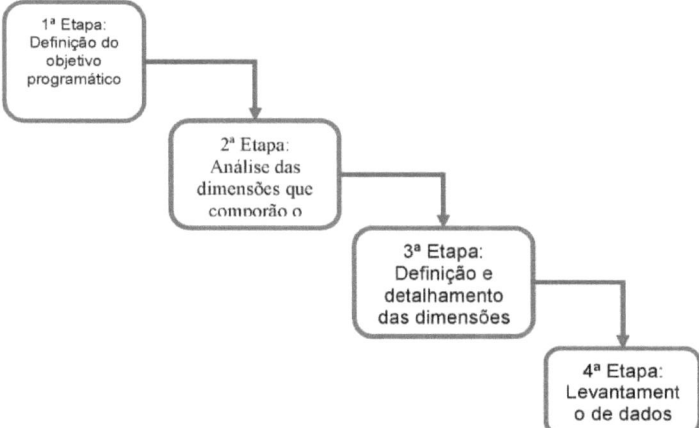

Figura 4. Methodology for constructing an indicator according to JANUZZI (2005). **Source:** The authors.

Results obtained

Based on the studies carried out in the previous items, the correlation of each analytical dimension of the indices presented was carried out, so that it is clearer which dimensions are considered most important, that is, which analytical dimensions appear in the indices.

The result shows varied economic performance in terms of sustainability levels among the municipalities of Mato Grosso do Sul from 2010 to 2015 values at both alert and ideal levels (Figure 5).

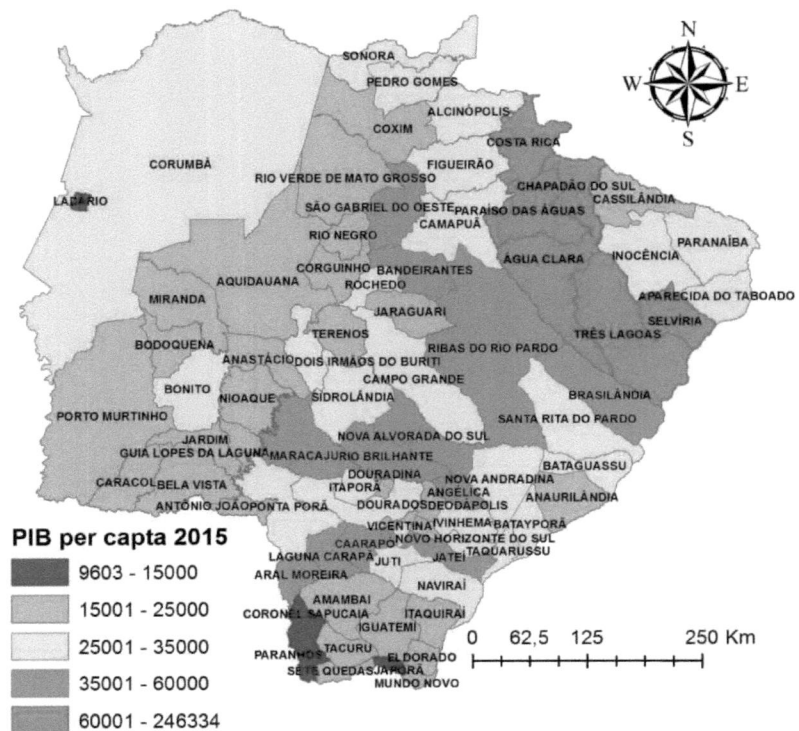

Figura 5. Map 1: Economic performance of Mato Grosso do Sul from GDP Per Capta 2015. **Source:** Elaborated from IBGE data (2017).

Based on the map it can be seen that no municipality was considered as ideal. This is due to the fact that there are municipalities that have a good economic performance, but in environmental or social terms are on alert.

By creating a ranking of the municipalities, the performance of the 10 municipalities of the state of Mato Grosso do Sul with the best results in Gross Domestic Product Per Capita in reais (R$) is verified with this total energy consumption and thus the average in relation to the individual economic performance of each one.

Table 2. Ranking of the top 10 municipalities with the highest Gross Domestic Product in Mato Grosso do Sul.

Municipality	GDP Per Capita in	GDP Per Capita in	GDP Per Capita in	GDP Per Capita in	GDP Per Capita in	GDP Per Capita in

28

	Reais (R$)	Reais (R$)	Reais (R$)	Reais (R$)	Reais (R$)	Reais (R$)
	2010	2011	2012	2013	2014	2015
Field Large	19.167,99	22.127,83	23.787,23	24.905,06	28.349,62	28.417,05
Dourados	19.204,78	24.190,67	27.244,31	27.098,98	33.101,70	34.219,12
Three Lagoons	38.507,63	42.418,40	47.997,58	59.237,51	64.528,84	69.184,36
Iguatemi	15.076,99	16.760,14	18.998,95	21.462,16	21.554,19	23.324,41
Paranaíba	15.220,51	17.157,88	18.431,51	21.174,03	24.464,35	26.619,77
Corumbá	17.960,14	20.315,15	23.319,64	24.829,00	28.712,25	25.154,17
Aquidauana	11.672,94	12.229,77	12.895,57	14.283,70	16.274,10	17.119,21
New Andradina	18.966,17	23.725,37	26.231,06	28.676,08	33.890,73	30.798,82
Bodoquena	17.542,69	20.330,36	21.521,41	22.575,77	24.044,41	24.926,20
São Gabriel do Oeste	28.420,77	31.280,51	41.858,48	43.315,81	49.148,07	55.056,06

Source: Survey data.

According to the results presented, Três Lagoas has the highest GDP per capita in reais. In the dimensions presented for the year 2010 it presented R$ 38,507.63 and in 2015 it increased its monetary variation to R$ 69,184.36. However, it can be seen that municipalities such as Campo Grande have a strong energy consumption in (MHW), but in terms of GDP per capita has performance considered below the largest municipality.

This shows that the environmental indicator can show the individual results for the municipalities, but the partial results of the indicators that make up the dimensions must be analysed in order to draw up appropriate strategies in the social, economic, institutional and environmental areas.

Table 3. Ranking of the 10 municipalities with the highest energy consumption in (MHW) in Mato Grosso do Sul.

Municipality	Total Energy Consumption (MWH) 2010	Total Energy Consumption (MWH) 2011	Total Energy Consumption (MWH) 2012	Total Energy Consumption (MWH) 2013	Total Energy Consumption (MWH) 2014	Total Energy Consumption (MWH) 2015
Field Large	1.312.735	1.394.232	1.519.280	1.613.104	1.742.866	1.752.247
Dourados	402.999	443.162	476.575	499.802	528.119	541.585
Three Lagoons	280.445	308.651	365.315	521.122	378.537	348.103
Iguatemi	17.862	16.582	20.897	22.674	23.011	24.891
Paranaíba	64.989	68.852	73.029	78.613	84.085	81.357
Corumbá	167.827	180.061	184.929	192.603	242.202	239.073

Aquidauana	60.526	64.083	70.360	71.924	77.200	75.705
New Andradina	78.391	78.850	86.833	102.517	110.112	104.323
Bodoquena	73.773	81.201	88.232	87.293	86.779	85.488
São Gabriel do Oeste	51.120	53.385	58.535	65.519	72.534	78.351

Source: Survey data.

According to the results presented, Campo Grande has the highest energy consumption (MWH). In the dimensions presented for the year 2010 it had 1,312,735 MHW and in 2015 it increased its monetary variation to 1,752,247 MWH. However, it can be seen that municipalities such as Iguatemi have a low energy consumption in (MHW).

The environmental indicator can show the individual results for the municipalities, but attention should be paid to the partial results of the indicators that make up the dimensions in order to draw up appropriate strategies in the social, economic, institutional and environmental areas.

Table 4. Ranking of the 10 municipalities with the highest average economic performance.

Municipality	GDP Constant Prices/ Total Energy Consumption 2010	GDP Constant Prices/ Total Energy Consumption 2011	GDP Constant Prices/ Total Energy Consumption 2012	GDP Constant Prices / Total Energy Consumption 2013	GDP Constant Prices/ Total Energy Consumption 2014	GDP Constant Prices/ Total Energy Consumption 2015
Field Large	16,89	16,47	15,49	15,08	14,47	13,84
Dourados	13,73	14,12	14,09	13,20	13,90	13,45
Three Lagoons	20,52	18,54	16,98	14,62	20,08	22,58
Iguatemi	18,46	19,72	16,82	17,13	15,35	14,65
Paranaíba	13,82	13,10	12,54	13,03	12,70	13,58
Corumbá	16,32	15,34	16,25	16,23	13,51	11,43
Aquidauana	12,93	11,39	10,34	10,91	10,45	10,66
New Andradina	16,21	18,18	17,48	16,11	16,24	15,02
Bodoquena	2,79	2,60	2,37	2,42	2,32	2,30
They are Gabriel do West	18,10	17,27	20,21	18,64	17,53	17,55

Regarding the economic performances in the ranking, Table 4 presents the results by the formula of GDP constant price divided by total energy consumption in (MHW) .

Analysing Table 4 we can see that Bodoquena has the lowest performance in relation to the behaviour of its economic actions. Sizing presents values in the year 2010 2.79 which resulted in a geometric mean of 2.42 the following years from 2011 to 2015. However, the ranking shows us that the city of Três Lagoas demonstrates a strong frugal performance in its financial activities, but in terms of the per capita dimension (R$) it has a performance considered narrow-minded oscillating from 20.52 to 22.58.

Therefore, in the analysis of the synthetic environmental indicator, the individual results for the municipalities are noted, however, the fractional repercussions of the indicators that make up the proportions should be analysed to draw up relevant methods in the social, economic, institutional and environmental areas.

Conclusion

The sustainable development effort in the state of Mato Grosso do Sul has been seeking to meet a guideline of the Federal Government of the Federative Republic of Brazil, starting to meet the disclosure of its information. As a result, accounting began to align its social and environmental financial data. This makes the southern region of Mato Grosso do Sul have its economic performance in a rational and sustainable manner.

However, in order to monitor this development and check whether it has been sustainable, the state proposes a system of environmental indicators, which, when integrated, form an extremely important tool for monitoring the policy of parsimonious progress.

It can be said, therefore, that when it comes to competitiveness in the state of Mato Grosso do Sul, Três Lagoas, alone, is the municipality with the highest average performance, presenting values of 20.52 in 2010 and in 2015 there was an increase to 22.52, followed by the group composed of São Gabriel do Oeste, Nova Andradina, Iguatemi and Campo Grande, which stand out in terms of competitiveness, all of them with financial performance within the range 13 to 16, being the most competitive, standing out from the other 79 municipalities in the state that have economic performance between 2 and 11, showing little competitiveness in relation to these first five.

As a conclusion, it is believed that this article has created a reliable and valid indicator, serving to signal trends and show the reality of competitiveness in the state of Mato Grosso do Sul.

However, it is hoped that it can contribute to the economic, social and environmental progression of Mato Grosso do Sul and can serve as an essential tool for its improvement, having great value in monitoring regional sustainable development.

Bibliographical References

CAMINO, R.; MULLER, S. Sustainability of agriculture and natural resources: bases for establishing indicators. San José: Inter-American Institute for Co-operation on Agriculture/Project **IICA/GTZ**, 1993. 133p.

CMMAD - **World Commission on Environment and Development. Our common future.** 2nd ed. Translation of Our common future. 1st ed. 1988. Rio de Janeiro: Editora da Fundação Getúlio Vargas, 1991. p. 27 - 99.

CARDOSO JÚNIOR, W. F. Inteligência empresarial estratégica: **Métodos de implantação de Inteligência Competitiva em organizações**. Tubarão: Editora Unisul, 2005. 176p.

CLAUDE, M. **Cuentas Pendientes: State and Evolution of Environmental Accounts in Latin America. Quito**: Fundación Futuro Latinoamericano, 1997. p. 8 - 16.

CORDANI, U. G.; MARCOVITCH, J.; SALATI, E. Evaluation of Brazilian actions after Rio-92. **Estud. Avançados**, São Paulo. v. 11, n. 29, p. 399-408, 1997.

IBASE - **Brazilian Institute of Social and Economic Analyses.** Available at: < http://ibase.br/pt/> Accessed on: 16 Sep. 2018.

IBGE. **Brazilian Institute of Geography and Statistics. Sustainable Development Indicators:** Brazil 2016. Rio de Janeiro: IBGE, 2016.

JANNUZZI, P. M. Indicators for diagnosis, monitoring and evaluation of social programmes in Brazil. **Rev. Serviço Público**, Brasilia, v. 56, n. 2, p. 137 160, 2005.

MARTINS, M. F.; CÂNDIDO, G. A. **Sustainable Development Index for Municipalities (IDSM)**: methodology for analysing and calculating the IDSM and classification of sustainability levels - an application to the State of Paraíba. João Pessoa: Sebrae, 2008. p. 1- 17

PEARCE, D. W.; WARFORD, J. J. **World without end: economics, environment, and sustainable development**. Washington: World Bank, 1993 p. 2 - 83

PEARCE, D. W. ATKINSON, G. Capital theory and the mesurement of sustainable development: in: Indicator of weak sustentability. Ecological Economics, 8 (2): 85-103. Measuring sustainable development, in BROMLEY, D.W. (ed.).1995. **Handbook of environmental economics**. Oxford: Blackwell.

PFITSCHER, E. D. **Accounting and social responsibility**. Florianópolis: Department of Accounting Sciences/ UFSC, 2009. P. 41 168

RAMOS, E. C. The process of constitution of the conceptions of nature: a contribution to the debate in Environmental Education. **Journal Environment and Education**, Rio Grande, v. 15, p. 67-91,

2010.

ROLDÁN, A. B.; SALDÍVAR-VALDÉS, A. Proposal and application of a Sustainable Development Index. **Ecological Indicators**, Mexico City, v.2, n. 3, p. 251-256, 2002.

ROMERO, M. A. B. A Sustainable Urbanism for the rehabilitation of degraded areas. **Research productivity report 2001-2004**, CNPq - UnB/ METRÔ DF, 2004. p. 47 -62.

SHIELDS, D.; SOLAR, S. MARTIN, W. The role of values and objectives in communicating indicators of sustainability. **Ecological Indicator**, Rio de Janeiro. v. 2, n. 1-2, p. 149-160, 2002.

TINOCO, J. E. P. KRAEMER, M. E. P. **Accounting and Environmental Management**. São Paulo: Atlas, 2006. p. 1078 - 1096.

WAQUIL, P. SCHNEIDER, S. FILIPPI, E. RUCKERT, A. RADOMSKY, G. CONTERATO, M. SPECHT, S. Evaluation of territorial development in four rural territories in Brazil. **Redes**, Porto Alegre. v. 15, n. 1, p. 104-127, 2010.

CHAPTER 7

General Conclusion

Mato Grosso do Sul is facing serious environmental problems. And the strength of sustainable development is reflected in the way that organisations have started to disclose their information. As a result, accounting began to integrate in addition to financial information, it also aligned itself with social and environmental data.

However, this research allowed us to determine the level of sustainable development of 79 municipalities in the state of Mato Grosso do Sul and to classify them according to their indicators. Coincidentally, it was possible for us to identify the best municipalities with the best level of economic performance in terms of sustainable development.

However, we present in a concise manner the main methods for measuring sustainable development indices and a history of the insertion of the environment variable in the recording of social and economic growth and development.

One of the purposes was the aid of accounting in the environmental management system, we were able to determine the indicators in the sense of sustainable development first by the historical aspect of sustainability, then in the indices and indicators and with this we formed the construction of these indicators with geometric mean.

From the use of this technique, we identified that only the municipalities of Três Lagoas, São Gabriel do Oeste and Nova Andradina presented results considered fully satisfactory in the sense of sustainable development. On the other side of the table, the municipalities of Bodoquena (2.30) and Aquidauana (10.66) are the municipalities with the lowest degree of sustainable progress.

A new challenge arises for accounting: the environment as an entity to be measured and controlled. Through economic and environmental information, monetised, it will be possible to determine a mitigation of the environmental impacts caused by human activities.

In view of this, we believe that these results can serve as a basis for the improvement of public policies in the municipalities of the state of Mato Grosso do Sul with the objective of promoting the growth of the sustainable development of these municipalities and, as a result, that of the state.